Anna Butterworth

Stylistic Harmony

ANSWER BOOK
Second Edition

OXFORD UNIVERSITY PRESS
Oxford and New York
1994

To Professor Ivor Keys

Acknowledgements

I should like to thank my colleague Philip Sawyer, at Napier University, Edinburgh, for his help and advice, and to express my deep gratitude to Pamela Brydon for her assistance in the preparation of the final manuscript. Many thanks go also to my husband, Neil, for his valuable proof-reading, and to Mrs Carol Crawford for patiently typing a complex manuscript with such care.

A.B.

OXFORD
UNIVERSITY PRESS

Great Clarendon Street, Oxford OX2 6DP
Oxford New York
Athens Auckland Bangkok Bogotà Buenos Aires
Calcutta Cape Town Chennai Dar es Salaam Delhi
Florence Hong Kong Istanbul Karachi Kuala Lumpur
Madrid Melbourne Mexico City Mumbai Nairobi Paris
São Paulo Singapore Taipei Tokyo Toronto Warsaw
and associated companies in Berlin Ibadan

Oxford is a registered trademark of Oxford University Press

First edition © Oxford University Press 1992. Second edition © Oxford University Press 1994.

Reprinted 1995, 1999

British Library Cataloguing in Publication Data
Data available

ISBN 0 19 321056 8

Designed by Fran Holdsworth

Printed in Great Britain

Contents

1. The Renaissance Period (*c*.1475–1600)   1
2. The Baroque Period (*c*.1600–1750)   17
3. Baroque Style:
   The Chorale   35
4. Baroque Style:
   Two- and three-part counterpoint   51
5. The Classical Period (*c*.1740–1815)   70
6. The String Quartet   84
7. The Early Romantic Period   93

1. The Renaissance Period
(c.1475–1600)

1 *Pange Lingua Gloriosi*: Office hymn

Phrygian

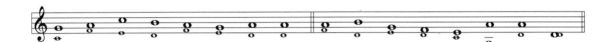

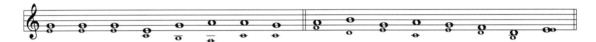

2 *Veni, Creator Spiritus*: Office hymn

Mixolydian

3 Thomas of Celano: *Dies Irae*, sequence in Requiem (13th cent.)

Dorian

4 Cantus firmus from *Aeterna Christi Munera*, Office hymn

Tactus = 𝅗𝅥

G:

5 Cantus firmus from *Christe Redemptor omnium*, Office hymn

Tactus = 𝅗𝅥

F:

x   x   x

6 Monteverdi: *Angelus ad Pastores* (1582)

Tactus = 𝅗𝅥

gau- di- um mag -   -   - numgau - di- um mag -   -   - num

F: gau - di - um mag -   -   - num gau - di - um mag -   -   - num

7 Lassus: Seventh Penitential Psalm (1584)

Tactus = 𝅗𝅥

Ex - pan - di ma - nus me -   as ad te:

G: Ex - pan - di ma-nus me -   as ad te: an - i-ma

[new point]

8 Lassus: *Magnum Opus Musicum* (1604)

Tactus = ♩

9 Ibid.

Tactus = ♩

10 Palestrina: Mass, *Aeterna Christi Munera* (1590)

Tactus = ♩

12 Morley: *I should for grief* (1595)

Tactus = ♩

13 Lassus: *Expectatio justorum* (1577)

15 Palestrina: *Exultate Deo* (1584)

16 Byrd: *Mass for Five Voices* (c.1595)

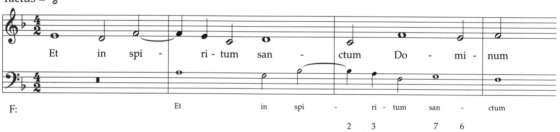

17 Redford: *Rejoice in the Lord* (from a keyboard piece in the Mulliner Book (c.1550–75))

18 Palestrina: Mass, *Aeterna Christi Munera* (1590)

19 Ibid.

20 Lassus: *Magnum Opus Musicum* (1604)

21 Ibid.

22 Tomkins: *When David heard* (1622)

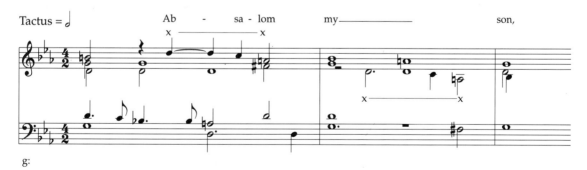

23 Tomkins: *Then David mourned* (? 1620)

24 Gibbons: *The Silver Swan* (1612)

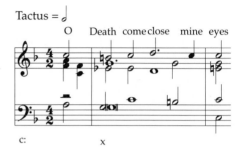

25 Dowland: *In Darkness let me Dwell* (1620)

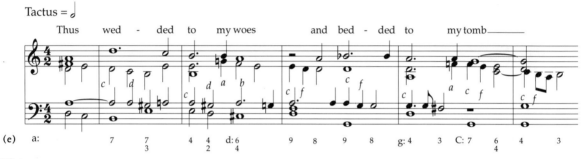

26 John Farmer: *Fair Phyllis* (1599)

27 J. Bennett: *All creatures now* (1601)

28 T. Ford: *Since first I saw your face* (1607)

Tactus =

Since first I saw your face I re-solved to hon - our and re - nown you

F:

29 J. Dowland: *Fine knacks for ladies* (1600)

Tactus =

Fine knacks for la - dies cheap, choice, brave and new, Good pen - ny

F:

worths, but mo - ney can - not move

30 Tallis: *Lamentations of Jeremiah* (? 1570)

Tactus =

Ie - ru - sa - lem, Ie - ru - sa - lem,

Ie - ru - sa - lem, Ie - ru - sa -lem, con - ver - te - re ad Do - mi - num De - um tu - um

F/d:

(Jerusalem, return again to the Lord thy God)

31 Lassus: Fantasia No. 1 (1577)

Tactus = ♩

d:

32 Lassus: Fantasia No. 3 (1577)

Tactus = ♩

G:

33 Lassus: Fantasia No. 5 (1577)

Tactus = ♩

g:

34 Morley: *Canzonets for Two Voices* (1595)

Tactus = 𝅗𝅥

35 Ibid.

Tactus = 𝅘𝅥

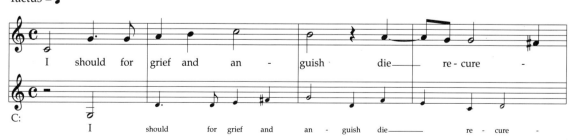

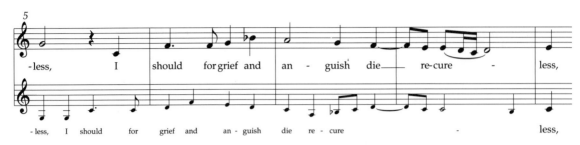

-less, I should for grief and an - guish die re-cure less,

- less, I should for grief and an - guish die re - cure less,

36 Ibid.

Tactus =

O thou that art so cru - el, My dain - ty love - ly jew -

C: O thou that art so cru - el, My dain - ty love - ly jew -

- el, My dain - ty love - ly jew - el, O thou that art so cru - el,

- el, My dain - ty love - ly jew - el, O thou that art so

My dain - ty love - ly jew - el, my dain - ty love-ly jew - el,

cru - el, My dain - ty love - ly jew - el, my dain - ty love - ly jew - el,

37 Byrd: *Mass for Four Voices* (c.1592–3)

Tactus =

Ag - nus De - i qui tol - lis pec - ca - ta mun -

g: Ag - nus De - i qui tol - lis pec - ca - ta mun - di

-di   mi - se - re - re,   mi - se - re - re,   no - bis

mi - se - re - re, mi - se - re - re, mi - se - re - re no - bis

38 Palestrina: Mass, *Aeterna Christi Munera* (1590)

Tactus = ♩

San - ctus, San - ctus, San - ctus.

San - ctus, San - ctus, San - ctus.

F: San - ctus, San - ctus,

39 Ibid.

Tactus = ♩

Be - ne -

Be - ne - dic - tus   qui ve - nit, qui   ve -

F: Be - ne - dic - tus   qui ve - nit,

- dic - tus   qui ve   nit,

- nit   Be - ne - dic - tus

qui ve - nit, qui   ve - nit

40 Weelkes: *Those sweet delightful lilies* (1597)

41 Morley: *Though Philomena lost her love* (1593)

42   J. Ward: *Fly not so fast* (1613)

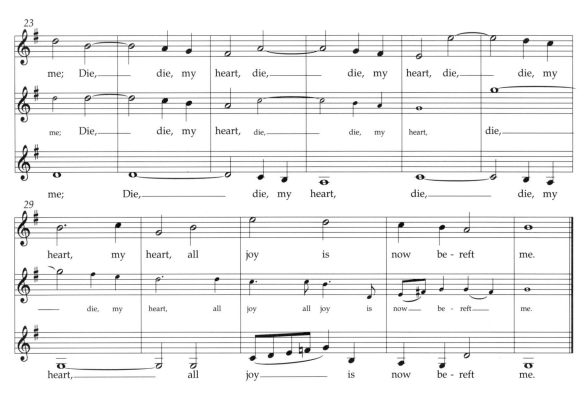

43 T. Tomkins: *Love, cease tormenting* (1622)

44   T. Bateson: *Phyllis, farewell* (1604)

2. *The Baroque Period*
(c.1600–1750)

45 Monteverdi: *Il ballo delle Ingrate* (1608)

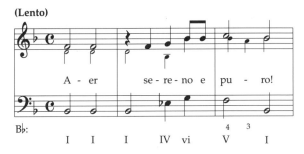

46 Schütz: *The Christmas Story* (1664)

47 Purcell: *Dido and Aeneas* (1689)

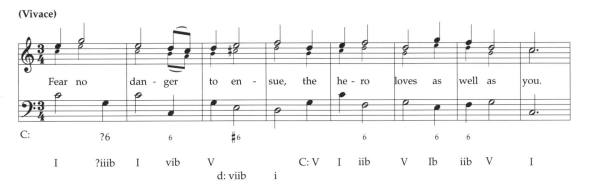

48   Purcell: *The Fairy Queen* (1692)

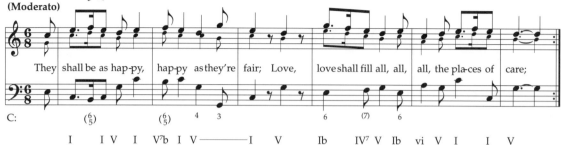

49   Purcell: *Remember not, Lord, our offences* (?1680)

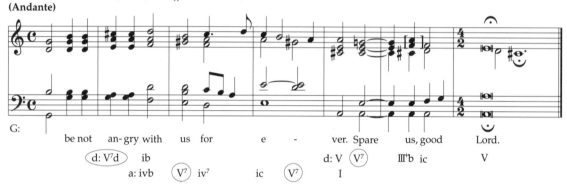

50   Monteverdi: Psalm, *Beatus vir* (1640)

(Blessed is the man that feareth the Lord)

51   Schütz: Symphonia from *The Seven Last Words* (1645)

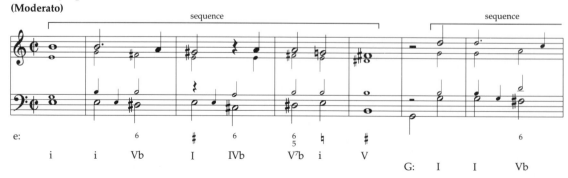

I   IVb   V⁷b I   V   D:Vb   I   Ib V   I   a:viib   I

53 Este's Psalter (1592)

F: V of d

         4 3   vi IV V   I
         x

54 Damon's Psalter (1579)

e: x   V of G

              4 3   x   4 ♯3
              x   x

                                                    i V   i

55 Melody from Este's Psalter (1592)

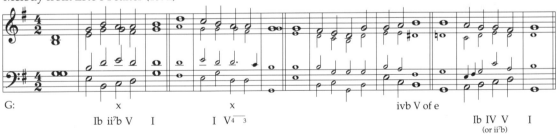

G: x   x   ivb V of e

   Ib ii⁷b V   I   I V⁴——³   Ib IV V   I
                                              (or ii⁷b)

56 J. Hilton: *Lord for thy tender mercies sake* (c.1594)
Tactus = 𝅗𝅥

F:

   Ib —— V vi IV V⁷   I

57 Bach: R. 24

G:

G: V⁷b I   iii
       D: vi ii⁷b V⁷   I

58   Mozart: *The Magic Flute* (1791)

C:

     V⁷b V⁷   vi   iib Ic V⁷   I

59   Schubert: Octet (1824)

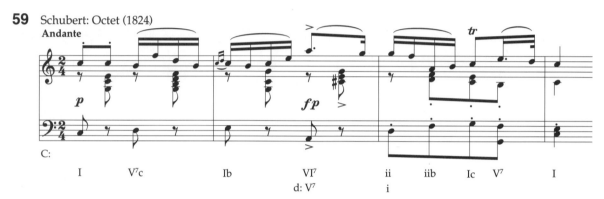

C:

   I   V⁷c   Ib   VI⁷   ii   iib   Ic V⁷   I

                    d: V⁷   i

60   Handel: *Messiah* (1742)

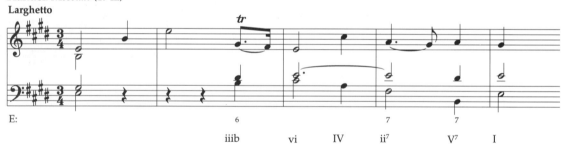

E:

              6   7   7

        iiib   vi   IV   ii⁷   V⁷   I

61   Purcell: *The Fairy Queen* (1692)   **62**   Bach: R. 242

Bb: e:

       IV   ii⁷ V⁷————I   i   II⁷b   V⁷   i

63   Corelli: Violin sonata Op. 5 No. 11 (1700)

E: Ib   IV   viib   iii   vib   ii   Vb   I

64   Ibid.

c♯:   i   iv⁷   VII⁷   III⁷   VI⁷   ii⁷   V⁷   VI   iv   V   i

65   Bach: Prelude No. 16, '48', Book 1 (1722)

c: V⁷b   i   iv⁷b   VII   ⁷   III⁷b   VI   ⁷   ii⁷b   V   ⁷   i

66   Corelli: Violin sonata Op. 5 No. 3 (1700)

C: Ib   IV   Ib   ii⁷   V⁷   I⁷   IV⁷   vii⁷   III⁷   vi

a: V⁷   i   vb   ivb   V

67 Purcell: *Ode for St Cecilia's Day* (1692)

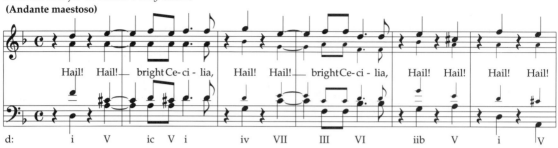

68 Bach: *St John Passion* (1724)

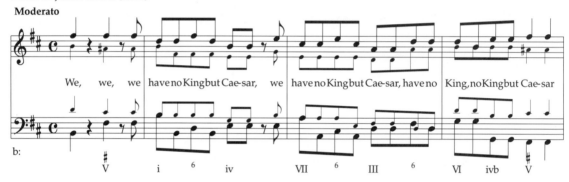

69 Vivaldi: Violin concerto Op. 3 No. 6 (1712)

70 Handel: *Zadok the Priest* (1727)

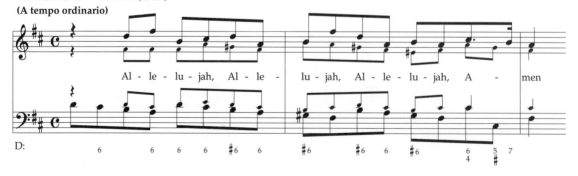

71 Handel: Suite No. 7 for Keyboard (*c.*1705–17)

72 Geminiani: Concerto Grosso Op. 3 No. 6 (1732)

73 Handel: *Jephtha* (1751)

74 Handel: Violin Sonata No.4 in D (*c.*1750)

75 Violin Sonata Op. 1 No. 6 (*c.*1730), attributed to Handel

Adagio

g: 6 4 #3   6   7 6   6 ♮6   # — 4 6 ♮6 4 7 #
                                            2   5   #3

*

76 Handel: *Messiah* (1742)

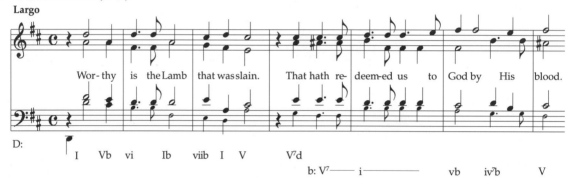

Largo

Wor-thy is the Lamb that was slain. That hath re-deem-ed us to God by His blood.

D: I Vb vi Ib viib I V   V⁷d

b: V⁷—— i   vb iv⁷b   V

77 Purcell: *The Fairy Queen* (1692)

(Moderato)

Vln. 1
Vln. 2

Cello
and
continuo

B♭: I ——— V ——— ii ——— vi ——— IV ——— IVb I   iii vi IV V I

78 Handel: Suite No. 4 for Keyboard (*c.*1733)

Courante

a: iv   [iib]   V⁷d——— ib ——— ic V   I V⁷ I

79 Monteverdi: *Il ballo delle Ingrate* (1608)

80 Purcell: *The Fairy Queen* (1692)

81 Corelli: Concerto Grosso Op. 6 No. 4 (*c.*1711)

82　Handel: Concerto Grosso Op. 6 No. 11 (1739)

A:

83　Bach: Fantasia in G minor BWV 542 (1717–23)

c:　　　　　　　　g:　　　　　　　d:

84　Bach: 'Fecit potentiam', *Magnificat* (c.1723 revised c.1728)

b:　　Men - te　cor - dis　su　　-　　i, men - te　cor - dis　su　-　i,

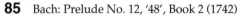

((He hath scattered the proud) in the imagination of their hearts)

85　Bach: Prelude No. 12, '48', Book 2 (1742)

A♭:

B♭:vii^{d7}　　I　E♭:vii　　I　b♭:vii^{d7}　　ib　vii^{d7}　　i

86 Bach: Prelude No. 14, '48', Book 2 (1742)

c♯:

b:vii^{d7} ib   c♯:vii^{d7} i   f♯:vii^{d7} i

87

c: ♭IIb V^7 i   g: ♭IIb ic V i   d: ♭IIb ♯iv^{d7} V i   a:♭IIb V i

88 Purcell: Canzona from *The Fairy Queen* (1692)

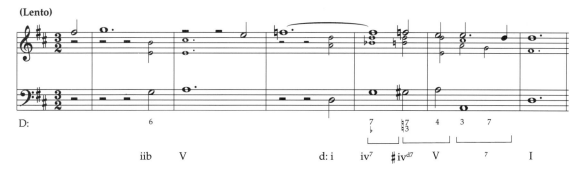

D:

iib   V   d: i   iv^7   ♯iv^{d7}   V   7   I

89 J. Stanley: Violin Sonata in G minor (?1740)

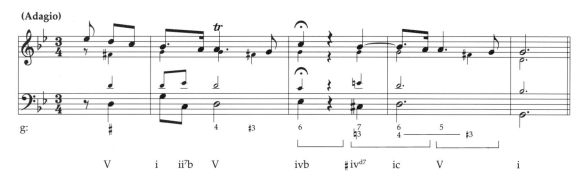

g:

V   i   ii^7b   V   ivb   ♯iv^{d7}   ic   V   i

90 Handel: *Zadok the Priest* (1727)

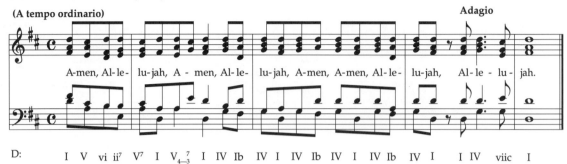

D: I   V   vi   ii⁷   V⁷   I   V₄—₃⁷   I   IV   Ib   IV   I   IV   Ib   IV   I   IV   Ib   IV   I   I   IV   viic   I

91 Violin Sonata Op. 1 No. 12 (*c.*1730), attributed to Handel

F:

f:

92 Purcell: *Jehova, quam multi sunt hostes mei* (*c.*1680)

(I lay me down and slept, then I awaked)

93   Purcell: Fantazia No. 2 in Four Parts (1680)

Note the use of III⁺b as a substitute for V

94   Bach: *St Matthew Passion* (1729)

((The griefs) how bitter yet how sweet are they!)

95   Handel: *Messiah* (1742)

(He was wounded for our transgressions, he was bruised for our iniquities!)

96   Stanley: Organ Voluntary Vol. 1 No. 1 (1748)

97   Stanley: Organ Voluntary Vol. 1 No. 5 (1748)

D:

98   Stanley: Organ Voluntary Vol. 2 No. 1 (1752)

d:

99   Handel: *Semele* (1743)

f:

(The death of Semele)

100 Purcell: *Dido and Aeneas* (1689)

101 Stanley: Organ Voluntary Vol. 1 No. 1 (1748)

102 Purcell: *Dido and Aeneas* (1689)[1]

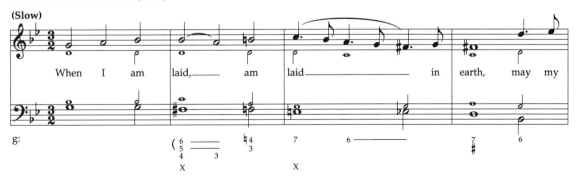

[1] The original is in five parts.

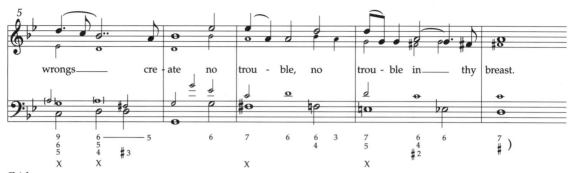

wrongs———— cre - ate no trou - ble, no trou - ble in——— thy breast.

103 Ibid.

(Slow)

104 Violin Sonata Op.1 No. 15 (*c.*1730), attributed to Handel

Largo

105 Bach: *St Matthew Passion* (1729)

(Moderato)

106   Handel: Concerto Grosso Op. 6 No. 4 (1739)

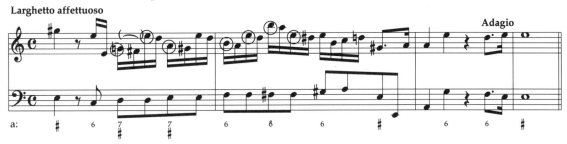

107   Purcell: *Dido and Aeneas* (1689)

(a) Chromatic writing: The slow descending chromatic movement of the ground bass is imitated by the upper parts in the closing ritornello of Dido's final aria, intensifying the already established mood of grief and tragedy.

(b) Dissonance: The tension is heightened by the use of suspensions; bars 6–12 include a dissonance on every strong beat. Note the effect of the diminished 4th (bar 5) and diminished 7th (bar 11).

(c) Rhythmic character: The smoothness of the rhythmic movement emphasizes Dido's dignified acceptance of her fate in spite of the anguish and despair she feels.

108   Handel: *Utrecht Te Deum* (1713)

(a) Chromatic writing: The 'sharpness of death' is suggested by the semitone movement, again descending and in imitation. Note the Purcellian repetition of the words 'sharpness' and 'of death', the latter preceded by a rest.

(b) Dissonance: Note the word-painting on 'sharpness', using a bass suspension (third beat of bar 2); also the unusual use of the augmented 6th chord (third beat of bar 3) and the diminished 7th chord (bar 4, second beat) both on the syllable 'sharp'.

(c) Rhythmic character: The repeated  rhythm accentuates the 'burden' of the words.

109   Bach: *St Matthew Passion* (1729)

(a) Chromatic writing: The angular line, a result of diminished interval leaps, fits the ugliness and menace of these words.

(b) Rhythmic character: The syncopated rhythm serves to pin-point the diminished intervals and to suggest the wild chant of the crowd.

3. Baroque Style: The Chorale

127　R. 14

G:

128　R. 40

C:

129　R. 48

a:　　　　　　　　II⁷b　V　I⁴　　³

130　R. 47

d:　　　　　　　#iv^{d7}　V　　⁷　　I

131　R. 71

e:

132　R. 15

g:　　　　　d: III⁺b

133　R. 151

G:
　　　I　Ib　V　Vb
　　　　e:vii^{d7}　i　　ib　　V

134　R. 3

G:
　　e: viib i　V　ib viib i　ivb　V

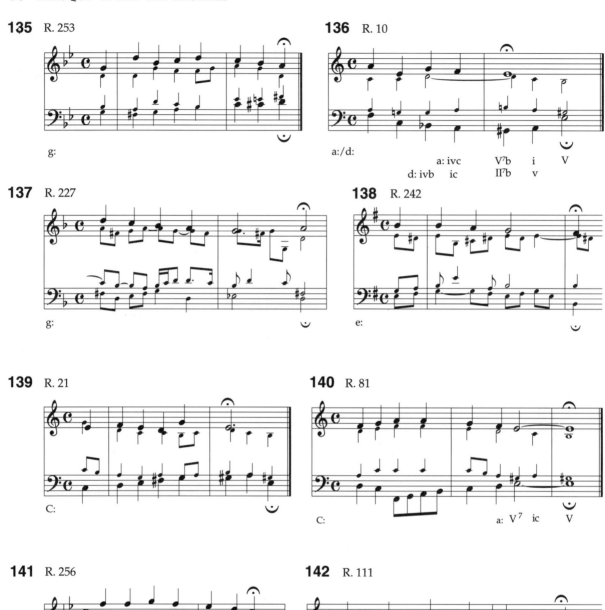

143 R. 179

Eb: 1*

144 R. 63

A: 2*   x

* Rare examples of: 1. a double suspension
                     2. double appoggiaturas

145 R. 358

g:

146 R. 283

e:

147 R. 143

F:

148 R. 231

G: x   x   x   x   x

149 R. 358

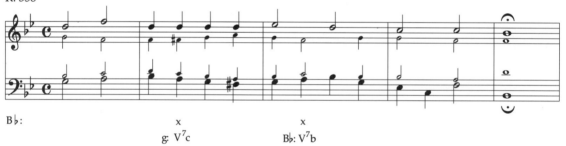

Bb: x   x
              g: V⁷c   Bb: V⁷b

150 R. 167

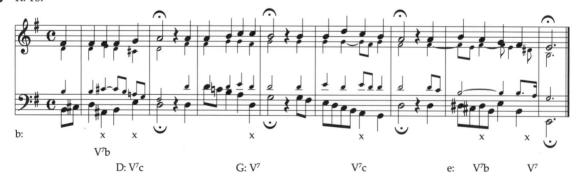

b: x   x   x   x   x   x
   V⁷b
        D: V⁷c   G: V⁷   V⁷c   e: V⁷b   V⁷

*R. = Number in the '69 Chorale Melodies with Figured Bass' in Riemenschneider.
[1] Editorial realization of figured bass. Not necessarily definitive.

156   *R. 59[1]

157   *R. 45[1]

[1] Editorial realization of figured bass. Not necessarily definitive.

158 R. 152

A:

159 R. 238

D:

160 R. 147

E♭:

161 R. 168

B♭:

¹ Editorial realization of figured bass. Not necessarily definitive.

[1] Editorial realization of figured bass. Not necessarily definitive.

173 R. 190

C:

I   V^4 a: i^9 $_6$ V^4 $_3$ $_4$ $_9$ $_8$

174 *R. 30

180 R. 21

a:

181 R. 105

e:

182 R. 115

D:

183 R. 73

g:

184 Bach: *St Matthew Passion* (1729)

f:

♭IIb

185 R. 13

d:

III⁺b

192   R. 170

4. Baroque Style: Two- and Three-part Counterpoint

193   Bach: *Italian Concerto* (1735)

194   Bach: *Little Notebook for Anna Magdalena* (1722–5)

195 Ibid.

196 Bach: *Six Little Preludes* (*c.*1720)

197 Bach: French Suite No. 6 in E (1722–5)

E:

198 Bach: French Suite No. 2 in C minor (1722–5)

199 Ibid.

Minuet

200 Handel: Suite No. 8 for Keyboard (*c.*1733)

Courante

201 Lully: *Le Bourgeois Gentilhomme* (1670)

(Moderato)

G:

202 Handel: *Water Music* No.8 (1717)

Hornpipe

F:

203 Ibid. No. 7

Bourrée

F:

204 Handel: Concerto Grosso Op. 6 No. 4 (1739)

Allegro

205 Handel: Concerto Grosso Op. 6 No. 8 (1739)

206 Telemann: Suite in A minor for Flute and Strings (*c.*1725)

207   Bach: Cantata No. 140 (1731)

208   'Herr Christ der einig Gottes Sohn'

209 'O Mensch bewein dein Sünde gross'

F:

210 'Nun komm, der Heiden Heiland'

a:

211 'Kommt hir zu mir'

g:

212 'Aus tiefer Not'

G:

213 Bach: *Nine Little Preludes*, No. 6 (1720–1)

g:

214 Bach: *Five Little Preludes*, No. 3 (*c*.1720)

e:

215 Bach: English Suite No. 5 in E minor (*c*.1715)

e:

216 Bach: English Suite No. 6 in D minor (*c*.1715)

d:

217   Purcell: *Ten Sonatas of Four Parts*, No. 9 (*c.*1680)

218 Ibid.

219 Purcell: *Twelve Sonatas of Three Parts, No. 2 (c.1683)*

220   Ibid.

221   Corelli: *Sonata da Chiesa* Op. 3 No. 1 (1689)

222 Ibid.

223 Corelli: *Sonata da Camera* Op. 4 No. 3 (1694)

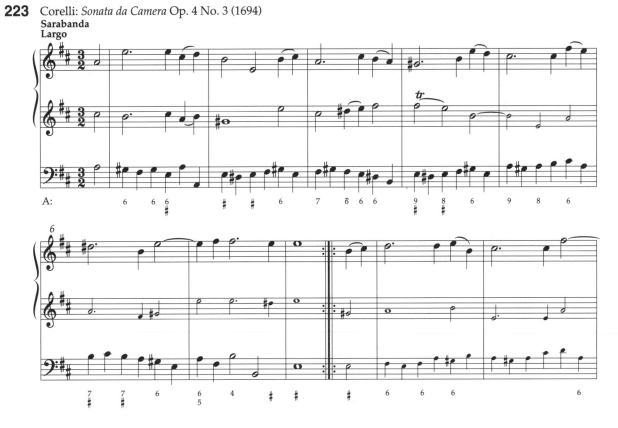

224 Corelli: *Sonata da Chiesa*, Op. 3 No. 4 (1689)

(cadence adapted)

225 Handel: *Water Music*, No. 17 (1717)

226 Handel: *Water Music*, No. 18 (1717)

227   Handel: Concerto Grosso Op. 6 No. 5 (1739)

228   Handel: Concerto Grosso Op. 6 No. 12 (1739)

5. The Classical Period
(c.1740–1815)

229 Mozart: Piano Sonata in C minor, K.457 (1784)

230 Beethoven: Symphony No. 5 in C minor (1807–8)

231 Haydn: *The Creation* (1798)

232 Haydn: String Quartet in D, Op. 76 No. 5 (1797)

F#: I IVc I V⁷ Ic V⁷ Ic V

233 Mozart: Symphony No. 40 in G minor (1788)

g: i ———————————————————— ii⁷d

234 Mozart: *Eine kleine Nachtmusik K.525* (1787)

D:

235 Beethoven: Piano Sonata in C minor, Op. 13 (1798)

A♭: V⁷d V⁷b (V) E♭:V⁷c

236 Beethoven: Violin Sonata in A, Op. 47 (1803)

237 Mozart: *The Magic Flute* (1791)

My own sweet maid or la - dy fair is Pa-pa-ge - no's plea; O such a sweet and

ten - der dove would be bliss e-nough for me!

238 Mozart: *Don Giovanni* (1787)

239 Beethoven: Piano Concerto No. 4 in G (1805–6)

e:

| V⁷d | a: V⁷b | G: V⁷ | e: V⁷ | V⁽¹³⁾₇ |

240 Mozart: String Quintet in G minor, K.516 (1787)

g:

241 Mozart: *The Magic Flute* (1791)

or let me die, or let_____ me die.

g:

242 Mozart: opening of the *Requiem* (1791)

d:

g:III⁺b   d:III⁺b

243   Mozart: Overture to *The Magic Flute* (1791)

E♭:

Ic ── V ── I

I V I V I V I V   I V I V I V I V   I

244   Haydn: *The Creation* (1798)

C:

245   Mozart: *The Marriage of Figaro* (1786)

C:

246 Haydn: 'Nelson' Mass (1798)

247 Beethoven: Symphony No. 9 (1822–4)

248 Mozart: *The Magic Flute* (1791)

249 Mozart: Clarinet Trio K. 498 (1786)

250 Beethoven: Piano Concerto No. 5, 'Emperor' (1809)

251 Beethoven: Symphony No. 6 (1808)

252   Mozart: Piano Concerto No. 17 in G, K. 453 (1784)

253   Beethoven: Violin Concerto in D (1806)

254   Mozart: *The Magic Flute* (1791)

255

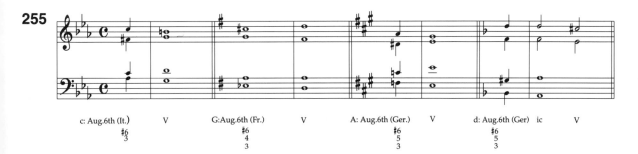

c: Aug.6th (It.)	V	G:Aug.6th (Fr.)	V	A: Aug.6th (Ger.)	V	d: Aug.6th (Ger)	ic	V
#6 3		#6 4 3		#6 5 3		#6 5 3		

256 Haydn: String Quartet in D, Op. 76 No. 5 (1797)

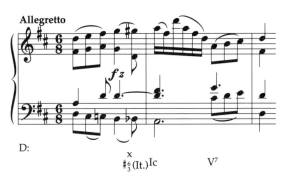

D:

x
#6 (It.)Ic   V7
3

257 Beethoven: Piano Sonata
Les Adieux, Op. 81a (*c.*1810)

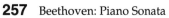

E♭:

x
c:#6 (It.)
3

258 Schubert: Symphony No. 9 in C (1828)

a:

x   x   x
(N6)
♭IIb   ic   V

259 Beethoven: Piano Sonata in
C♯ minor, Op. 27 No. 2 (1801)

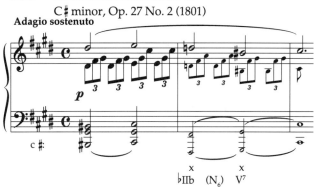

c♯:

x   x
♭IIb   (N6)   V7

260 Mozart: Clarinet Quintet in A, K. 581 (1789)

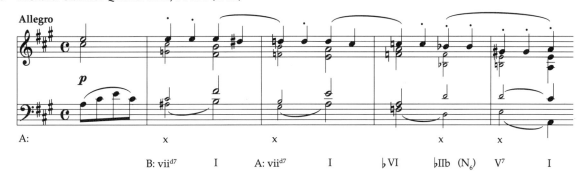

A:

x   x   x   x
B: vii d7   I   A: vii d7   I   ♭VI   ♭IIb (N6)   V7   I

261   Mozart: Divertimento for String Trio in E♭, K. 563 (1788)

262   Haydn: *The Creation* (1798)

263   Mozart: *The Magic Flute* (1791)

Hours of   joy   for e - ver   vanish'd, nought my   hope   can now re - store

264   Haydn: Symphony No. 88 in G (?1787)

265 Beethoven: Symphony No. 3 in E♭, 'Eroica' (1803)

Adagio assai: Marcia Funebre

266 Mozart: 'Lacrymosa', *Requiem* (1791)

(Ah! that day of tears and mourning! From the dust of earth returning, man for judgement must prepare him!)

(a) *The melodic line*

The melody line on the word 'lacrymosa' (='weeping') rises a minor 6th only to fall back. The ascending scale that follows moves diatonically (bars 5–6) and then, as the tension increases, chromatically (bars 7–8) to a chilling climax, a warning of impending judgement. These were reputedly the last bars that Mozart wrote before he died.

(b) *The accompaniment figures*

Detached crotchets in the bass (♩ ⁷♩⁷) move the music inexorably foward, while the 'sigh' figure of the opening (⁷♪♪ ⁷♪) shadows the melodic line throughout, adding touches of dissonance.

(c) *The use of rests*

The 'sigh' figure is an important element setting the atmosphere for 'Lacrymosa'. The use of rests to indicate the 'catching of the breath' or a sigh may be seen in earlier music, e.g. Tomkins: 'Weep no more' (1622). See Workbook, p. 15.
The rests at bars 5–7 in the chorus parts evoke a fearful, expectant response in the listener.

(d) *The harmonic language*

(i) The shifting harmonies, with rapid modulations from bar 5, add to the sense of unease and tension, and help to build the climax at bar 8.

(ii) The appoggiatura (C♯) and the telling cross relation in bar 1 (fourth beat) are devices long associated with the 'affect' of grief; similarly

(iii) The diminished triad (bar 3, third beat), the diminished 7th (bar 7, fourth beat), the dominant minor 9th (bar 3, fourth beat), and the augmented 6th (bar 8, second beat), chords.

6. Classical Style: The String Quartet

267 (a) The legato bowing conveys the unruffled nature of this music where the only 'ripple' is the *mf p* in the cello line. The passage is quiet, but there is a sense of forward movement created by the 'portato' chords repeated in the accompaniment which support the smooth dialogue between the cello and the first violin.

(b) The texture creates a sense of spaciousness due to the wide intervals between the outside parts while the role of each line is clearly perceived by the ear.

268 (a) The importance of the bowing is again demonstrated in this extract where it conveys both the light grace () in bars 1–8, and heavier humour ( ) in bars 9–13. Accents (>) and the *fz* signs add sudden contrasts.

(b) The melody line in bars 1–8 has a light, sparse accompaniment helped by rests. The texture becomes thicker in the louder bars (9–13), and the new idea from bar 14 involves a quiet, graceful melody in octaves in the first and second violins accompanied by a light figuration in the viola and cello.

269 Mozart: String Quartet in D minor, K. 421 (1783)

270 Ibid.

271 Mozart: String Quartet in C, K. 465 (1785)

272 Haydn: String Quartet in F, Op. 17 No. 2 (1771)

273 String Quartet in C, Op. 3 No. 2 (formerly attributed to Haydn)*

274 Haydn: String Quartet in C, Op. 9 No. 1 (*c.*1769)

*Op. 3 is now believed to be by R. Hoffstetter (1742–1815). See Alan Tyson and H. C. Robbins Landon, 'Who Composed Haydn's Op. 3?', *The Musical Times*, July 1964.

275   Mozart: 12 Duos, No. 9, K. 487 (1785)

276   Mozart: 12 Duos, No. 10, K. 487 (1785)

277 Mozart: 12 Duos, No. 11, K. 487 (1785)

278 String Quartet in C, Op. 3 No. 2 (formerly attributed to Haydn)

279 Haydn: String Quartet in B♭, Op. 33 No. 4 (1781)

280 Haydn: String Quartet in F minor, Op. 20 No. 5 (1772)

281 Haydn: String Quartet in B♭, Op. 2 No. 6 (?c.1761)

282   String Quartet in F, Op. 3 No. 5 (formerly attributed to Haydn)

C:

283   Ibid.

F:

284 Haydn: String Quartet in C, Op. 9 No. 1 (*c.*1769)

285 Ibid.

Menuetto
Poco allegretto

286   Haydn: String Quartet in C minor, Op. 17 No. 4 (1771)

7. The Early Romantic Period (c.1810–50)

287 Schumann: *Dichterliebe*, No. 5 (1840)

The li - ly shall faint - ly e - cho A

a: i ———————— ib ———— iv°⁷ ———— VII⁷ ———— III⁷ ———— VI⁷ ————

song   of this love   of   mine.

ii⁷   ib   iib   ♯iv^d7   V

vii^d7b

288   Schubert: Symphony No. 5 (1816)

289   Mendelssohn: Overture, *A Midsummer Night's Dream* (1826) (outline)

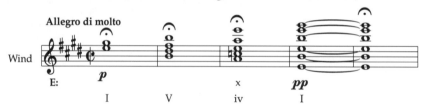

290   Schumann: *Dichterliebe*, No. 7 (1840)

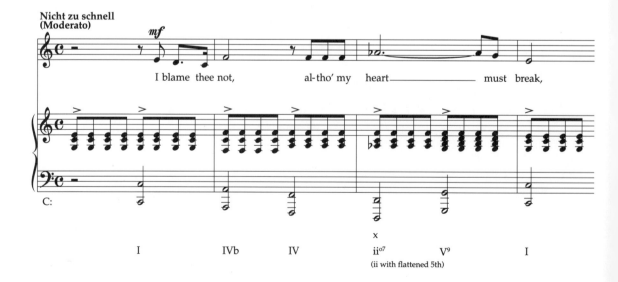

291 Schumann: *Album for the Young*, No. 43 (1848)

292 Chopin: *Ballade*, Op. 47 (1841)

A: ii   #i°b   iib———   Ic   V⁷   I
         = viib of ii

Ab: I   III⁷   vi   V⁷   I
         =V⁷ of vi

293 Wagner: *Siegfried*, (1871)

Ab: V   V⁺   ♮iv°⁷   V⁷d   Ib   V⁷c   I   II⁷c   Ic
         =vii⁷ of V   =V⁷c of V

294 Wagner: *The Valkyrie*, (1856) (Valkyrie motif)

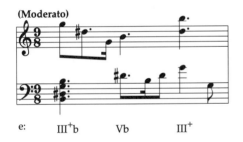

e: III⁺b   Vb   III⁺

295 Schumann: *Dichterliebe*, No. 8 (1840)

f#:   x
                           ♭IIb

Tis she   who caused   my   sor-row,   And broke   my heart in twain.

296   Wagner: *Tristan and Isolde* (1859)

G:

d: ivc   vii^{d7}   i   ♭IIb   V

297   Schubert: Octet in F (1824)

298   Wagner: *Tristan and Isolde* (1859)

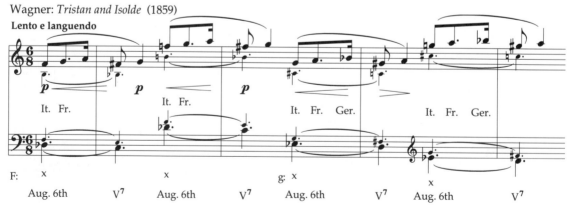

299 Liszt: Piano Sonata in B minor (1853)

D:

accompagnamento

b: V¹³(c)

300 Mendelssohn: Octet for strings (1825)

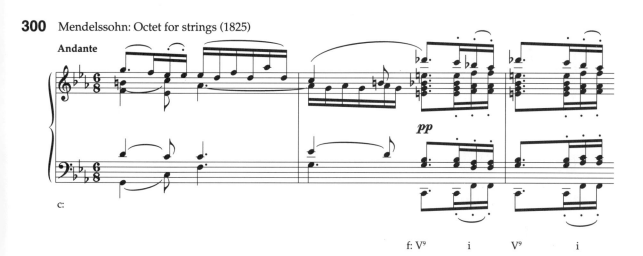

c:

f: V⁹   i   V⁹   i

301 Mendelssohn: *Song without Words* Op. 53 No. 2 (1841)

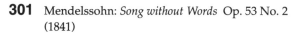

a♭:

V¹¹

302 Wagner: *The Rhine Gold* (1854) (sword motif)

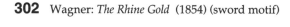

C:

V¹³

303   Schumann: Piano Concerto in A minor (1845)

a:

Unprepared dissonance occurs at climax of phrase to maximum effect.

304   Schumann: 'Valse noble' from *Carnaval* (1835)

B♭:

Unprepared dissonance occurs at climax of phrase to maximum effect.

305   Berlioz: *Les Nuits d'Été* (1834–41)

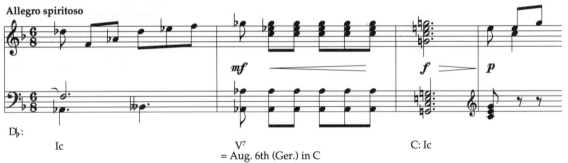

D♭:

Ic   V⁷   C: Ic
= Aug. 6th (Ger.) in C

Pivot modulation — augmented 6th used as a pivot chord.

306   Schubert: Quintet in C (1828)

G: V   (Viola)
                                       E♭: I

Abrupt modulation — moving onto a note which then takes a tonic role.

307 Chopin: Mazurka Op. 56 No. 1 (1843)

B:

B:＿＿＿＿   A:＿＿＿＿   G:＿＿＿＿

Modulation by sequence.

308 Schubert: Ländler (?1821)

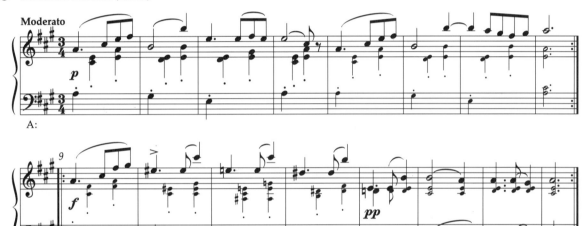

A:

309 Chopin: Nocturne Op. 62 No. 2 (1846)

E:

310 Schubert: Impromptu Op. 142 No. 3 (1828)

311 Chopin: Mazurka in A minor, Op. 7 No. 2 (1830–1)

312 Schubert: Octet in F (1824) (outline)

313 Ibid.

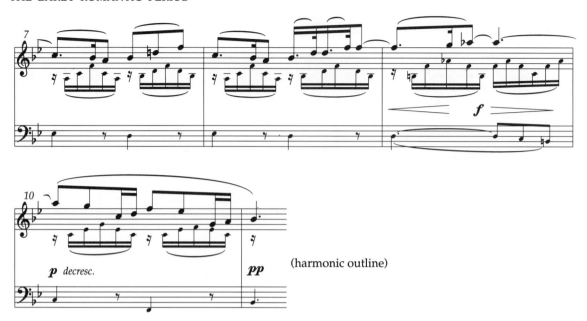

(harmonic outline)

314 Schubert: Quartettsatz in C minor (1820)

(harmonic outline)

315 Schubert: Fantasia in F minor, D.940 (1828) (Outline*)

* The original is for piano duet (four hands).

316 Schubert: 'Der Wegweiser' (The Guide Post) from *Winterreise* (1827)

317 Schubert: 'Die Neugierige' (The Enquirer) from *Die schöne Müllerin* (1823)

318   Schubert: 'Gretchen am Spinnrade' (Gretchen at the Spinning-wheel) (1814)

319 Mendelssohn: Terzetto (The Angels) from *Elijah* (1846)